SMITTEN

BY

KITTEN

How to Buy, and Look-after

your first Cat

Jamie Boyd

Dedication

This book is dedicated to Toby, Bailey and Maisy, treasured friends who have made my life more pleasurable.

Contents

Introduction

CATS.

Creatures that have both mystified and charmed humans for centuries.

Worshipped as divine by the ancient Egyptians, seen as good luck symbols by the Japanese, and used as rodent-catchers by multiple civilizations down through the ages.

So, *who* or *what* are these strange creatures that so bewitch and delight us with their magic and cuteness?

Who can resist the allure of a kitten? A tiny soft ball of fur staring at you with that innocent, wide-eyed look that just pleads, "Love me!"

Of all the things in this world that can so easily captivate the human heart, a small fluffy kitten seems to be right up there near the top of the list. Appealing to our most basic human instinct to protect the weak and helpless, they pull us in like a tractor-beam, with their innocent eyes peering into the very depth of our souls and tugging at our heartstrings.

Once a kitten looks into your eyes, you are gone: hopelessly smitten by a helpless kitten. You know that you have no choice: she has decided your fate for you. You *will* be bringing her home. She has made sure of that!

But what happens next? What do you do, once your heart gets trapped by one of these siren-like creatures? What if you have never owned a cat before? How are you going to look after her? What will she need? What is she going to eat? Where is she going to sleep? What is it all going to cost?

Luckily for you, this book is here to answer all those questions. We are going to look at all the concerns you might have about owning your first cat and try to answer all the "What?"s, "How?"s, and "Why?"s going through your mind.

We will look at where to buy a cat, how to choose one, and what things to look out for.

We will look at the things you need to buy before bringing your cat home; and how to look after them once you do.

We will look at how to help your new best friend become familiar with their new surroundings and how to help them blend-in to become part of your family.

We will look at what veterinary care they will need in their first year, what medications they will need, and what general care you will need to give them.

We will also look at some typical feline behavioral problems and how to overcome them.

By the end, you should have enough knowledge to feel confident about entering the world of cat ownership for the first time.

Who am I? Well, I am just like you! I am someone who had never owned pets before and had no idea how to look after them. I never had family pets at home when I was growing up (apart from a couple of short-lived goldfish). So, on becoming a pet owner as an adult, I had to learn everything firsthand.

In order to look after my own pets, I have had to learn everything about pets and pet-care for myself, reading, researching, and learning by trial-and-error to find out everything I am sharing here with you.

My own story is that my father never wanted pets around the house. In his childhood, he had grown up in a home that had a cat, but he didn't like it and didn't want to have animals around his own house. So in *my* childhood, I grew up without knowing the comfort and joy that having a pet can bring to a household.

My wife, on the other hand, had grown up having many pets around and loved the idea of having pets of her own. So she was much keener to have pets after we got married and settled down to our life of marital bliss. We did own a dog for a few years in the early days, at my wife's insistence. Still, I generally resisted getting other pets because I was just not used to it and always regarded it as discomfort and a burden to have animals to look-after around the home.

We eventually got our first cat when our kids were young, despite my misgivings. We only had it for a few years, and for some reason, I never really bonded with it. It was only after many years when my wife and daughter insisted that we get another cat, that I finally found myself magically transformed into a pet lover.

On acquiring our current feline, I found that I quickly grew to love her. I found that I had discovered what an absolute joy having a pet can be. It was a total revelation to me one day to realize that I cared about her and loved having her around. Now, I can safely say that I would thoroughly recommend anyone to get a cat, and I would never be without a cat in the home. I see the presence of a cat as a real benefit to the mood and behavior of everyone in the family. Your cat becomes a true member of your family and teaches all of you how to love, how to be gentle, and how to care.

In short, I have become a real advocate of owning pets, and I believe that getting a cat will transform your home and bring so much love and peace into your life.

If you haven't thought about getting a cat before, let me encourage you to take the plunge and dive into the highly rewarding world of cat ownership. You have nothing to lose and so much to gain. I promise you will not be sorry!

Chapter 1

Why a Cat?

> *"There are two means of refuge from the
> miseries of life: music and cats."*
> **Albert Schweitzer**

HOW MANY TIMES have you thought about getting a pet? How many times have you thought about having a small creature to love and care for? How many years have you been longing for a steady companion to share your life with?

Interacting with other human beings is good and necessary; no-one should be going through life without family and friends to love and be loved by. But having a pet to interact with is an altogether different kind of relationship.

With a pet, you can develop a friendship that is constant despite everything else. It is a reliable, trustworthy bond that is always there. When the world around you starts getting crazy, it doesn't matter what love or acceptance you are getting or not getting, from anyone else around you, because your furry friend loves you no matter what. It is a special love that is always there waiting for you at home, an unspoken trust, where both of you know that you are just *there* for each other.

You know what it is like: you come home from a long day at the office feeling exhausted and misunderstood, and you drop onto the sofa exasperated. You wish that a meteor would crash onto your workplace overnight so that you never have to go back there again. You start entertaining fantasies that your mean ugly boss would meet some untimely, gruesome end. Then your cat climbs up onto the sofa, sits down in your lap, and rests her paw on your hands. At that moment, you know that everything will be alright. The world stops being a scary place, and you start to relax.

Now, I know that there are many types of animals that can make wonderful pets; dogs especially can be great companions, but cats are uniquely suited to be that special kind of friend to you. Their very nature is soothing and calming, and their ability to snooze, wherever and whenever, lets you know that it is okay just to let go and relax. Their lovability and cuteness factor provides a focal point in the home for love to be expressed. Indeed, the presence of a cat in the home can bring out the soft side of even the hardest of hearts.

Benefits of owning a cat

There are many benefits of having a cat in the home, not just to your general wellbeing, but also to your physical health.

Companionship – as already stated, cats are great as companions. They are very loyal and affectionate, and depending on the breed, they will follow you around the house as your ever-present shadow, moving from room to room as you do. If you live alone, you will definitely not feel alone with a cat around.

Psychological Health - Cats are great listeners. Owning a cat is like having your own therapist on-hand at all times. You can pour your heart out to a cat, telling them all your woes - and feel like you have genuinely communicated with another being. And they won't answer back or argue the point; their presence just reassures you that everything will be okay.

In fact, one Australian study concluded that cat owners actually have better psychological health and less incidence of depression than non-pet owners.[1] In other surveys, cat owners reported themselves to be happier, more self-confident, and able to focus better and feel more able to handle problems in their lives than non-cat owners.

10 | P a g e

Healthier Heart – there have been scientific studies that show that stroking a cat can lower your blood pressure and reduce your heart rate.[2] Not only that, but cat owners have a lower incidence of cardiovascular disease in general, and cat ownership is also associated with a lower risk of dying by a heart attack. Wow! Those are some great benefits!

Healthier Bodies – when a cat purrs, the purring vibrations are at a frequency of between 25 and 150 Hz. Some studies have shown that this can be beneficial in helping strengthen and heal fractures in bones.[3] 25-50 Hz is the ideal frequency range, with 100-200Hz also being effective. The purring vibrations also supposedly help soft tissue injuries to heal in muscles and tendons, as well as helping to reduce inflammation. It appears to be part of an internal self-healing mechanism in cats themselves, but it is thought that it could also be beneficial to us humans. Listening to a cat purr is, at least, very relaxing.

Fewer allergies – a 2002 study by the US National Institute of Health showed that having dogs or cats in the house for the first couple of years of a child's life meant less likelihood of developing allergies.[4] By having pets in the home, the children's immune systems seem to develop in a way that prevents them from developing reactions to common allergens.

That last one is surprising to me because cats are traditionally associated with having some people being allergic to them. But due to my own experience, I think there must be something in it.

As I previously mentioned, I grew up without any pets in my home; and I suffered from asthma as a child and was allergic to cats. Even as a young adult, whenever I visited homes that had cats, I would react with a runny nose and shortness of breath. I once had a reaction just from sitting in a friend's car for 5 minutes because there was some cat hair on the seats. However, somewhere along the line, that all changed.

We got our first cat about 15 years ago because my eldest daughter longed for one. Despite my initial trepidation, I found that as soon as I got used to having the cat in the house, my allergy subsided. Although we only had that cat for a few years, I seemed to adapt to having it around. I never really had any allergic reaction to it, despite still being asthmatic to some extent, and I have been fine with cats ever since then.

With our current feline family member, I can spend all day with her and nuzzle her right up in my face without experiencing any reaction whatsoever. So I can only assume that having spent time around cats, I have lost the allergic sensitivity and developed a tolerance for them.

How long do cats live?

The expected lifespan for a domestic pet cat is at least 15 years. In the wild, cats might only live for 2 to 5 years due to the harsher conditions and susceptibility to predators. But, when a cat lives in a human household, life expectancy increases dramatically. So when you get a kitten, you are adopting a new family member that will be around for quite a while. You may even have your cat for up to 19 or 20 years if they manage to live to such a ripe old age.

In the past, I often heard it said that cat and dog years were equivalent to 7 human years; but it turns out that it is not strictly true. A cat's age cannot simply be multiplied by seven to get an equivalent human age because they develop at different rates in different stages of their life when compared to humans.

Cats develop very quickly when they are young. The first 12 months of a cat's life are like 15 human years. Then the second 12 months are equivalent to 9 human years. So a two-year-old cat is like a 24-year-old human. After that, the rate slows down more and each cat year is roughly equivalent to 4 human years.

So the relationship between cat and human ages goes like this:

Cat age – Human age

Cat age		Human age
1 month	→	1 year
3 months	→	4 years
6 months	→	10 years
1 year	→	15 years
2 years	→	24years
3 years	→	28 years
5 years	→	36 years
10 years	→	56 years
15 years	→	76 years
20 years	→	96 years

Chapter 2

Which breed should I get?

"The smallest feline is a masterpiece."
Leonardo da Vinci

CATS come in many different shapes and sizes. Everything from the mighty African Lion to the tiny Singapura miniature is considered a type of cat. But only some types of cats are suitable to be kept as pets because obviously, you can't have a large wild cat roaming your house. Or can you?...

Unbelievably, there was a trend for a little while in the 1970s where it became "hip" for people to keep big-game cats in their homes as pets. As Western society emerged from the heady days of the 1960s and tried to make sense of the upheaval to societal norms that had happened in the decade of free love, people were looking for different ways of living in an attempt to define the "new normal." Both in the UK and the United States, people were buying all kinds of exotic wild animals to keep in their homes illegally. This trend lasted for a few years until the authorities clamped down and put a stop to it.

In London, there was the famous case of Christian the Lion. Christian was purchased as a cub from Harrods in Knightsbridge and raised in a flat in Chelsea. His owners used to take him out on trips, driving around London in an open-topped car, much to the amazement of wide-eyed onlookers. But obviously, this was far too dangerous, and also completely impractical, as Christian grew very large, very quickly. Eventually, they made the wise decision to have him shipped off to Africa and released into the wild.

It was a sad day for them to let him go, as they had formed such a strong bond with him. But, amazingly,

Christian was not going to forget them. When they visited him in the wild many years later, he recognized them instantly by their smell and started licking and hugging them like a long lost friend. They say that elephants have a long memory, but this is an excellent example of the loyalty and companionship that is possible with a feline.

As much fun as it might seem, though, to have an African Lion or a Bengal Tiger lounging around on your sofa, you clearly don't want to be eaten by your pet cat in your own home. So for our purposes, we need to look at something a little smaller. We need to look at what are considered the "domestic" breeds of cat.

How many Domestic Breeds?

How many domestic breeds are there? Well, that depends on who you ask. Several official organizations classify cat breeds. They base their classification on different criteria, such as genetic ancestry, body type, length of coat, etc.

Since these various organizations each classify breeds slightly differently, they differ in their agreement of the total number of domestic breeds. For example, the International Cat Association recognizes seventy-one breeds, whereas the US-based Cat Fanciers Association only recognizes forty-four breeds.

Whichever way you look at it, that is still a lot of breeds to choose from. So, where do you start when choosing a cat as a pet? Well, it's easiest just to look at the most *popular* breeds out of the list and consider only those that are most commonly kept as pets in the western world.

Top 10 Popular Domestic Breeds

The popular breeds all have their different appeal. They all have different looks and colors and temperaments to consider. And they have different levels of maintenance required. For instance, if you choose a long-haired breed, they are going to molt heavily and require a lot of brushing, etc., whereas a short-haired breed is going to have a coat that is much easier to maintain.

The following were the Cat Fanciers Association Top Breeds in 2019. They are ranked below by their popularity among cat owners that year.

1. Ragdoll

Ragdolls have become very popular in recent years. They are a beautiful gentle-natured cat, excellent for having around children. They are called ragdolls because of their tendency to relax and flop when you pick them up, just as if they were a lifeless rag doll. They have a placid nature and don't mind being handled slightly roughly by small children. They have a long coat, which is usually white with smoky-colored head and tail and paws (colorpoint).

2. Exotic Shorthair

The Exotic Shorthair is a cross between the American Shorthair and the Persian breeds. It has become immensely popular in North America over the last few years. A very affectionate and playful cat, the Exotic has a much shorter coat than the traditional Persian, which makes it more appealing due to less grooming time required.

3. British Shorthair

One of the most recognizable types of cat, the British Shorthair, is often used in advertisements selling cat food, etc. Note, the Cheshire Cat in Alice in Wonderland was a British Shorthair. As well as having that classic cat look, they have a beautiful plush coat, thick and soft like a cashmere blanket. They have been around for a long time; it believed that they were initially introduced to Britain in the first century by the Romans. They make an ideal house-cat, as they have a calm, relaxed temperament that makes for a great companion. Their coat can be tabby or colorpoint but is more usually a color known as Blue. Which is not actually blue, but a beautiful deep gray color which shines with a rich blue-ish hue, especially when seen in the sunlight.

4. Persian

Instantly recognizable as the beautiful white Snowbell in the Stuart Little movies, the Persian has always been a popular breed. The classic long-haired cat that likes to sit in stately luxury and be pampered, they are very affectionate and easy-going. They are the oldest known breed, having been around since early biblical times. If you want a Persian, though, be aware that you are going to be brushing that beautiful long coat every day, and you may even have to bathe it once in a while to make sure it stays clean.

5. Maine Coon Cat

The Maine Coon is natural to North America and is the largest breed of domestic cat. They can grow to weigh more than 20lbs as an adult, but despite their size, they are gentle-natured and generally intelligent and playful. Almost dog-like in nature, they respond to having their name called and like to be played with. Their appearance is a little more "rugged" than other breeds as they have a rough-looking shaggy coat and a long tail.

6. Devon Rex

The Devon Rex is a curious-looking cat with a unique appearance. This breed was discovered in Devon in south-west England only in 1960, but has quickly found its way into the hearts of cat lovers everywhere due to its quirkiness and mischievous behaviour. Its unique look is mainly due to its large alien-like over-sized ears that make it look a bit like a bat. They have curly hair and long legs, and are very inquisitive, liking to explore and play.

7. American Shorthair

Brought to America by early settlers in the Pilgrim days, this cat is an easy-going all-rounder highly suitable as a family pet. They have a nicely-defined facial structure, which makes them appear open and friendly. They are gently playful and get along with other pets easily. Their short hair makes them low-maintenance and ideally suited for a young family.

8. Abyssinian

Abyssinians are very beautiful, graceful-looking cats. They have long slender bodies and a more pointed shaped face, with large ears. They are the closest to the classic Egyptian-looking cat. When you look at one, you can just imagine them sitting there next to Cleopatra. They are not ones for sitting in your lap, but they are very interactive and like to join in with whatever activity is going on around them.

9. Sphynx

The Sphynx cat is a strange-looking beast. If you don't want to be brushing and grooming all the time, then the Sphynx may be your answer because they are hairless. Some Sphynx's do have a light peach-fuzz type of coat, but others are totally bald. The lack of a decent coat means they have to be kept indoors to be protected from the elements, but they are warm to the touch and smart enough to cuddle-up if they do get a bit chilly. They love people and like to play and have a reputation as attention-seekers that always want to interact with you.

10. Scottish Fold

A relatively modern breed from Scotland, so-named because their ears appear folded-over forwards, rather than standing up straight. This feature makes them the most adorably cute-looking of all kittens, and they retain this cuteness in their facial features as adults. These cats are curious because they love to make lots of different meow-ing and purring sounds, which gives them a reputation as "talkers." They also like to sit back in a chair in a human-like pose, with their back legs out front and their front paws resting on their tummy.

Types of Coat

When looking at Domestic Cats breeds, one thing to note is that they all come in various types of coloring or coat patterns, which are used to describe each particular cat. The most common coat patterns are:

Solid – one even color all over, e.g., white, black, cream, chocolate or gray.

Tabby – meaning they have a striped, spotted or swirled pattern of two colors. All Tabby cats have a distinctive "M" shaped stripe pattern on their forehead

Colorpoint – meaning they have one main color all over, but a different color on their extremities (or points) such as the tail, face, ears, and legs

Tuxedo – one color on the top, which can be solid, tabby or colorpoint; but with a white underbelly extending up to their chin or face. As the name suggests, it looks like the cat is wearing a tuxedo suit jacket over a white shirt.

Choosing

The breed that you choose is entirely up to you. The type of look you like, the personality, the coloring, etc. are all very personal choices that you need to consider according to your preference in regards to what your idea of the perfect cat is.

Your choice may be dictated, to some extent, by what cats are available when you are looking for one. You may like a particular breed but find there are none available in your local area at that time. In that case, you need to decide whether to wait for a new litter to be born, or whether to choose a different breed that is more readily available.

But, at the end of the day, any breed of domestic cat is going to make a wonderful addition to your home and family.

You won't need to walk them as you would a dog, and even a higher-maintenance cat is going to require less work than most other pets. And you can't beat the loyalty, love, and companionship that your new feline friend is going to give you.

Chapter 3

How and where to buy your cat

"Cats choose us; we don't own them."
Kristin Cast

WHEN YOU BUY A CAT, it usually happens one of two ways: either (a) it is carefully planned, or (b) it is totally spontaneous.

One of those ways happens when you research breeds and look into what type of cat you want, start talking to breeders or shops in your local area and wait for a litter to be born and weaned.

The other way, which, let's face it, is more likely, happens when you walk past a pet shop and see a cute face staring at you in the window. Before you know what has happened, you find yourself sitting at home on the kitchen floor with a new kitten on a blanket, wondering what to feed her and where she is going to sleep!

Don't worry; we have all been there and done that, captured by the forlorn gaze of a lonely animal in a pet-store window. But if you can manage it, the best way to expand your family into pet ownership is to plan for it properly.

However, even when you *do* plan for it, there is still a right way and a wrong way to go about buying a cat

The Wrong Way

The "wrong way" includes: answering a classified ad in the local paper, buying a cat out of the back of a truck at the market, and even taking a free kitten off somebody-who-knows-somebody at work.

You can tell I am not a fan of these cat buying methods. Why? Well, because you just don't know what you are getting and putting it bluntly, you are often being duped. It is highly likely that someone is taking money off you to offload a cat that they have been unable to sell via a legitimate channel for some reason.

A cat that is acquired in any of these ways is, more than likely, going to have some kind of problem. You just don't know what it is yet, so you don't know what hassle you are getting yourself into.

Diseases are common, but of more concern are poor quality cross-bred animals that have some kind of genetic abnormality that causes health problems later on.

What you need to consider is that when you purchase a cat, you are investing two things: you are not just investing money; you are also investing your heart. So you need to ask yourself, "Do I really want to get myself emotionally attached to an unhealthy animal that I am going to have to watch suffer later on?"

And it will cost you financially too. If you think you are saving money by buying a cat cheaply, you are

SMITTEN BY KITTEN

not. It is a false economy. Once your heart is invested, and you have formed a loving bond with your new best friend, you are going to want to do whatever you can to help them if and when they get sick. And expensive vet bills are the price you will have to pay for skimping on the initial cost of a good quality animal.

A final point to consider here is the effect it can have on your children. When you bring a pet home, it becomes a member of your family. Your children bond with it, and it becomes their best friend. But if that beloved family pet was never healthy in the first place and gets sick or dies after just a few months or even a couple of years, it can be very traumatizing. You can avoid all that heartache by doing the right thing in the first place.

In my opinion, even picking up a cat from the local Pound is preferable to the options above. Although once again, you do not know what you are getting, and with a "Pound cat," you could be bringing home an animal with behavioral issues.

The Right Way

The "proper way," or at least a *better* way, to buy a cat, is to buy from a breeder, or a reputable pet shop, or even from your local vet.

Breeder - Cats from breeders will come from healthy stock. They will be genetically sound and have no abnormalities that can cause problems as the cat grows. Most States or jurisdictions have certification processes for Breeders, with specific standards and requirements that the Breeder needs to meet. This guarantees that you get a healthy kitten that has the best chance of growing up strong and won't develop issues once it is an adult. Buying a cat from a breeder is more expensive initially but is worth it in the long run. You ensure for yourself that you are getting a healthy animal that has the best chance of a long, happy life. Your family deserves that.

Pet Shop - Cats from Pet Shops should be the same, as long as you go to a well-established decent-sized store.

Larger shops usually get their stock directly from breeders. They will establish good relationships with many reputable local breeders to ensure that they always have a constant supply of healthy stock for their store.

You should be able to tell where the stock is coming from just by talking with the staff in the store. Just ask how many weeks old the cat is and how long the cat has been in the store, and you will start to get an understanding of where it has come from. You will often see a whole litter of the same animal in the store when the stock has come from a breeder.

Beware, though; not all pet stores are the same. Small, independent stores should be okay in general, but beware if a store seems to be showing signs that it is struggling. In such cases, they might not be buying quality stock from breeders and be getting any animals they can from less reliable sources. When this is the case, you usually find that they might only have single animals rather than a litter, and generally only a few animals in the whole store.

Vet – not always the first thought that comes to mind for most people, as we tend to think of vets as places to "fix" pets rather than acquire them, but your local vet may often have animals for sale. And if not, they will at least be able to point you in the right direction. Talking to your local vet is undoubtedly the easiest and quickest way to get useful information about the supply of pets in your local area. They will know who the good breeders are and which pet shops are the best for getting quality animals. Chatting with a vet is definitely a good information gathering exercise to do before you decide where to buy.

The Pound – As mentioned earlier, I am in two minds about buying a cat from a Pound or Pet Shelter. On the one hand, you show yourself to be a good citizen by adopting an unwanted animal with no home. It is all very altruistic and certainly helps society, and I understand that is a good thing.

But on the other hand, you don't know why they have ended up in the shelter, and often they may have behavioral issues. Adopting a mature cat is a very different experience than adopting a kitten, and you need to be prepared to "take what you get," just as you would when adopting a teenage child. So if you get a mature cat from a Shelter, you need to be ready for what may be a wild ride as they adapt to a situation that may be very different from what they are used to. It may be a while before they fully settle into their new home environment.

I also understand that for many people, when funds are short, getting a cat from a Shelter may be the only economically viable option. So if you *do* buy from a shelter, just ask as many questions as possible and try to find out as much as you can about that particular pet and their background. That will hopefully help you avoid bringing home a cat with issues.

How old?

Once a litter of cats is born, the kittens stay close to their mother, being dependent on her for milk, warmth, and comfort. But by about eight weeks, the kittens will have been weaned and be eating solid food.

Ideally, they should then stay with the mother for a few more weeks to keep growing and become more confident. Kittens are growing very rapidly at this stage, and every few days that pass are equivalent to a few months of human growth.

This eight to twelve week period is like the toddler stage for humans; and although we might put our toddlers in nursery or childcare for a few hours whilst we work, we don't usually start sending our kids off to spend a full day at primary school until they are past that toddler stage. The same with kittens, it's good for them to start playing and exploring away from their mother at this age, but they are a bit young to leave her and be adopted by a human family, just yet.

So if you are buying from a breeder, try and arrange to leave them with the breeder until twelve weeks, even if you already have arranged the purchase. However, you can't do that with a pet shop kitten as the kittens will have already left their mother. It is quite common for kittens to arrive in pet shops at around nine or ten weeks. And I think that is okay; after all, pet shops need to make money, and it's easier to sell kittens the smaller and cuter they are. But I just think that overall, it is better for their all-round social development if they don't leave their mother and go off alone to start their new independent lives until they reach twelve weeks.

How to select a cat

"Which one do I choose?"

That is a big question.

- What should you look for when selecting a cat?
- How do you know which one is going to be the best?

The main thing you want to look for when choosing a kitten is Personality. Cute looks are fine, but at the end of the day, you need a cat that you feel a connection to and want to spend time with.

Whatever the situation, either at the breeder's home or the pet shop, you should have a chance to look at the litter and interact with them when trying to choose one. Look for one with an open personality: one that is playful and inquisitive, but not too rambunctious. You want to find the middle ground between not too aggressive and not too shy or timid.

If you can, get down on the floor to be at the same level as them. See whether one naturally comes to you. Try and offer them a toy to see if they are not too shy to reach out and take it, and play with them a little. Try caressing them on the top of their head with the back of your hand.

After a few minutes, pick them up. See if they are happy to let you hold them without struggling to get away or bite you.

While you are doing this, be asking questions of the breeder or shop assistant. Try and find out as much as you can about the kittens' history and find out what the seller has already noticed about each kitten's particular personality.

Once you find a kitten that you seem to connect with, check it over to make sure it looks healthy. You obviously won't know *too* much about cat health yet, but just be aware of any obvious signs of anything, like patches of fur missing or any rashes or scars. Note whether they look too fat or too skinny compared to others in the litter; a healthy kitten should be neither. Feel their tummy and make sure that it doesn't feel hard or swollen, which could indicate worms. Run your finger through their fur and check for fleas etc. Take your time; don't rush the process. Remember, you are going to have this pet in your family for many years to come.

When you find the right one, though, you will just "know" it. They say it is as much about the cat choosing you as it is about you choosing them, and once they have chosen you, your heart is going to feel it.

Chapter 4

Things you need to buy

"Cats seem to go on the principle that it never does any harm to ask for what you want."

Joseph Wood Krutch

WOW! CONGRATULATIONS on choosing your new furry friend! A wonderful new stage of your life is just about to begin. But now you have found the companion of your dreams, what next?

Well, you need to consider how you are going to look after them and what things you are going to need to make them feel comfortable. Soon we will need to look at how to prepare your home to welcome them, but first, it's time for everyone's favorite pastime …it's time to do some shopping!

There are obviously some essential items you are going to need to enable you to look after your new pet. If you haven't owned a cat before, it's unlikely that you are going to have these things already lying around your home, so you are going to have to go out and spend some money. But the good news is that you don't have to spend too much money!

When you start looking in stores at pet-care items, you are going to come across are some things you will definitely need and some other things that you probably don't need. You can buy those other things if you want to, but you don't really have to. Just getting the basics will be more than adequate as a first-time cat-owner.

Things you DO need

The following items are essential purchases when you become a cat owner for the first time. This is the essential Top 10.

Pet Carrier

A good sturdy pet carrier is essential to be able to safely transport your new best friend. You are going to need it before you pick up your new pet to take them home for the first time, and after that, you are going to need to use it for trips to the vet, for check-ups, etc.

These days they are available in a variety of styles, in both soft-collapsible and hard-plastic versions. Personally, I would recommend the hard-plastic type as I feel they are much safer. If you had any kind of traffic incident whilst you were traveling with your pet in the car, a sturdy hard plastic carrier is going to offer much more protection than a soft-collapsible nylon/canvas type of carrier.

It does not have to be expensive; Pet Carriers are a fairly cheap purchase these days. You can pick up a decent quality item from as low as twenty dollars from most homeware stores. If you opt for the soft canvas type of carrier make sure the zips are positioned out of reach of the pet so that they can't enact an escape!. If you choose the hard plastic-type, make sure you get one with a spring-loaded door latch, as they tend to be more secure.

Food and Water Bowls

You are going to need bowls to put out food and water for your kitten. I actually recommend getting three bowls rather than just two. You need one for water obviously, but I like using two for food. One bowl for "wet" food, i.e. meat, that you use just at mealtimes, and one for dry food that you can leave out all day as a "grazing" bowl.

You should avoid plastic bowls as plastic deteriorates over time and can eventually harbor bacteria. Instead, get either ceramic or stainless steel bowls, as they can be washed easily and will last forever.

Food

Your initial food purchase will be most likely be according to the advice of the pet shop or breeder that you are buying the animal from. Your kitten will be used to eating a certain type of food, and you will want to maintain that for the first couple of weeks, at least. Your kitten will be going through enough other changes as it gets used to living in a whole new environment with you, so keeping their food the same for a while will help them cope better with that transition to their new home.

The shop or breeder should be able to supply you with a batch of the type of food the kitten is already used to, which will be a good quality kitten food. It might cost you a little more to buy it off them, but as a one-off purchase, it is much easier to do that than running around town looking in different stores trying to find the same brand and flavors on the day that you pick your kitten up to take them home. You can then work out where to buy that food more cheaply later on, and even change the food gradually after a few weeks if you want to.

I like to feed a kitten both wet and dry foods: a small amount of a good quality meat product in the morning and evening and have some dry food (kibbles) available for them to graze on throughout the day. You could feed them just the dry food if you want to. As long as it is labeled as a "complete kitten food," it will contain all the nutrients and vitamins that are necessary to satisfy them and keep them healthy. They need to have kitten food for the first 12 months; then, they can transition to adult cat food in their second year.

Litter Tray and Liners

A litter tray is a must. Even if you have made the decision to allow your cat outside and are hoping they will use the garden for all their business, you will still want to maintain a litter tray inside the house for those times when your cat decides not to go outside to answer the call of nature. A simple plastic litter tray is all that is required, nothing more complicated, and I suggest getting a pack of plastic Litter Tray Liners. Liners make it much easier to empty and clean the tray and stop the tray itself from getting too smelly. Cat urine can stain and erode the plastic tray over time, so tray liners help to keep urine off the tray itself.

Litter

There are many different types of cat litter available these days, and each has its benefits. But once again, it is best to stick to the kind your kitten has been used to so far, at least for the first few weeks. You don't want them to get confused in their new environment and start urinating outside of the tray.

So start with the same type that the pet shop or breeder has been using. Then, after your kitten has settled in for a few weeks, you can change them over to a different litter if you really want to. But if you do, you will need to make that change as a gradual process. Start by adding a just scoop or two of the new type of litter into the tray along with the old type of litter. Then over a period of a few days, gradually increase the ratio of new to old until you are fully using the new type.

The main types of litter sold today are:

Clumping Clay Litter- granules of natural clay that clump together when wet, allowing you to remove urine-soaked lumps easily.

Recycled Paper Litter- grey pellets made of recycled newspaper, which goes dark when wet.

Crystal Litter- small rock crystals of white translucent silica which are highly absorbent.

Natural Litter- environmentally-friendly products made from a whole variety of different natural substances. They are usually pellets made from pine, wheat, corn, or other natural biodegradable substances. My local store is even selling litter made from Soy and Tofu!

Bed

Your kitten will need somewhere cozy to settle down and sleep. Cats are notorious for being able to sleep anywhere, especially on your favorite armchair, but they do need somewhere of their own that they can identify as their special place to rest.

Pet beds come in all shapes and sizes, but I would recommend getting a soft igloo or cube-type that your kitten can go inside to escape from the outside world. Cats love going into covered spaces, getting underneath anything they can squeeze themselves under, so having a covered cube type of bed gives them a secure "nest" they can curl up in.

Brush

Some cats are going to need a lot of brushing, others not so much. Longhairs, you will be brushing pretty much every day, shorthairs occasionally – a hairless Sphynx not at all!

A good quality wooden-handled brush is worth buying, but even cheaper plastic-handled brushes from your local homeware store are of decent-enough quality these days and will do the job.

Nail Clippers

If you don't like getting scratched, you are going to need to clip your cat's claws. This is especially important if you have small children. Kittens may look cute and harmless, but the first time they climb up the outside of your pants leg, you suddenly find out just how sharp their claws are!

There are several styles of clippers available for cat's claws: some use a scissor action, others use a guillotine-type action. If you are not sure what to get, you can try using regular human nail clippers if you want to, but they are more fiddly to use. You will need to clip your cat's claws regularly every couple of weeks, so you want to get clippers that are comfortable and easy to use. Note, you can get your vet to clip them on your initial health-check visit. You can see what type they use, and ask them to show you how to do it correctly.

Scratching Post

Even though you clip your cat's claws, they will still need something to "scratch" on. If you don't have something available, they *will* scratch on your furniture. Scratching is a natural instinct that serves several purposes. It keeps their claws in good shape by shedding the outer dead layer; it helps them stretch themselves after a big nap, and it allows them to mark their territory by leaving their scent from glands in their paws. Ideally, you should purchase a scratching post that is about 3 feet or one meter high, so that is taller than the cat when they stretch out.

Another option to consider here is a cat climbing tree that includes scratching posts. That may cost a little more, but probably not too much more. And it serves the dual purpose of giving your cat a perch to climb up onto as well as somewhere to scratch their claws.

Cat Toys

Every kitten needs a toy. The classic image of a kitten playing with a ball of wool exists because kittens are playful. Sure, they sleep a lot of the time, but during their waking hours, they need stimulation and something to keep them occupied.

You should get two or three toys so that there is a variety. They will need toys that you play with them and toys that they can play with on their own. Kitten playtime is all about learning the art of hunting, so they like things they can chase and catch, mimicking the movement of a mouse or a fish. Simple toys like a plastic wand with a shape on the end of a string provide wonderful ways to get a kitten moving and chasing around after the shape as you drag it around the floor. And toys with bells are great for calling your kitten out from a hiding spot when you can't find them.

Things you DON'T need

There are also many items that you *can* buy if you want to, but in my opinion, they are unnecessary. The list of products being produced for pets is endless and increasing every day. People love to spend money on their pets, and manufacturers are constantly putting out new products to try and grab a bigger share of the market.

Don't get me wrong. I am not *against* purchasing any of these items; I just don't think you don't *need* to, especially if you are on a budget.

The following is a list of the most commonly available products that are out there waiting to swallow up your hard-earned cash. Whether you *do* buy any of these is entirely up to you.

Cat Shampoo

Cats are naturally self-cleaning animals, so bathing them is not really necessary. They lick and groom themselves regularly to keep their coat clean, but there is a limit to how much they can cope with.

There may come a time, however, when your kitten gets a little too over-enthusiastic with exploring and gets covered in mud or even cream from that cake you just finished making. If that happens, no amount of licking and grooming is going to cut it, and you might have to bathe them, in which case you would need cat shampoo. But so far, this has never happened to me.

You can also get Dry Shampoo for cats, which is a powder that you can shake onto them and brush through their coat.

Toothbrush and Toothpaste

Okay, so this is a tricky one. Cats can get plaque and tartar build-up just like humans, and they can get periodontal gum disease too. So, vets do recommend brushing a cat's teeth daily, or at least a few times a week. But in my opinion, it is not really necessary.

Now you might think I am a bad cat owner, but I must admit I have never brushed my cat's teeth. When I spoke to my vet about it, she admitted that she had never brushed any of her cats' teeth either.

If you do want to do the right thing, then you can purchase a cat toothbrush, which is a small silicon rubber brush that fits over your finger, along with some cat toothpaste. Or instead of a cat toothbrush, you could use a small mini-toothbrush designed for a human baby. Don't use human toothpaste, though; it will not be good for your cat.

Cleaning Wipes

Cat cleaning wipes are a pet-friendly version of baby wipes. To be honest, these could be handy. If your cat has got themselves dirty and you don't want the hassle of trying to give them a bath, you might be able to just give them a wipe-over and avoid all the pain.

These can also be useful if your cat has an injury, or is incapacitated in some other way, and is prevented from being able to bend and reach everywhere that needs cleaning. So these are useful, but not necessary unless your cat cannot clean themselves.

Catnip Sprays and Deterrent Sprays

These sprays seem to be available at every pet shop nowadays. They are designed to entice your cat towards things you want them to touch or play with (catnip sprays), or discourage them from touching things you don't want them to go near (deterrent sprays).

Personally, I find the smell of these sprays quite off-putting for myself, and I'm not a cat. In general, I don't like introducing unnecessary chemicals into the home environment, and I am especially wary of introducing anything that might be an irritant. Use them if you want, but monitor your cat to see if the sprays are upsetting them.

Fancy Litter Trays

There are so many different types of fancy litter trays available now. There are trays with lids, trays with doors, trays disguised as other objects, and trays built into furniture. There are even electronic "self-cleaning" litter trays! But really, who needs that? Why spend three hundred dollars on a litter tray when you could spend three dollars?

I also see some drawbacks in having covered litter trays. For one, because you can't easily see the litter, you are more likely to be oblivious to how dirty it is getting and forget to change it. And secondly, since cat urine is smelly, fumes can build-up inside the box. If it gets too smelly in there, your cat will not want to go in to use it.

So my advice is to go the old-fashioned route and use a straight-forward rectangular plastic tray. Using plastic litter tray liners is as fancy as you need to get with a litter box.

Automatic Feeders

Automated electronic feeders are another gadget available in the marketplace. But do you really want one? Part of your interaction with your cat is feeding time. You feed them each day, and they grow to rely on you. Why would you want to replace that special part of the relationship with an automated feeder?

The only possible use I can see for one of these is if you are not able to be home for a particular feeding time. You should not be using them to feed your cat on a regular basis or whilst you are away for a few days.

If you are going to be away, you should either be getting someone else to feed and check on your cat; or take them to a cat boarding facility.

What is all this going to cost?

I really don't think you should spend any more than you need to on the essential Top 10 items. As with everything, there are two ways to buy: cheap or expensive. But as long as they are functional and fit for purpose, I see nothing wrong in buying cheaper items from a homeware store rather than paying top dollar at specialized pet stores. This is especially true when you are just starting out as a pet owner and don't yet know what things you might want more expensive versions of.

Having said that, I can hear my Father's words of wisdom ringing in my ears: "If you buy cheap, you buy twice!"- meaning that a cheaper version of something may not be of the quality required and will need to be replaced much sooner than a more expensive version would have.

But my own experience has shown me that for some things, the more expensive item is not always the best quality one. So my advice is: for everything, look at it, examine it, and compare it. If you can't see that the quality-difference is worth the price-difference, then save your money and buy the cheaper one!

Chapter 5

Prepare Your Home For Baby

"Time spent with cats is never wasted."
Sigmund Freud

P REPARING YOUR HOME to welcome a new kitten is very much like getting ready to welcome a new baby into the home. After all, your little kitten *is* a baby. Yes, it may only be a baby animal, but it needs a safe environment to grow in, just like a human baby does.

If you were bringing home a human baby, you would be looking at your home, removing any hazards, and putting certain things out of harm's way. You would be finding a safe place to put their cot, away from loud noises and bright lights. You would be working out where to keep their food and nappies and toys and generally preparing the home ready to receive them. Bringing home a kitten is no different.

Look for Possible Dangers

Go around your home, starting at the front door, and look at everything as if you are a visitor seeing your home for the first time. It is surprising what you see when you look at things from this perspective.

Things that are normally invisible to you because of familiarity suddenly stand out as in need of obvious attention. Look for clutter that needs to be put away. Look for anything that could potentially fall over if knocked. Look for anything that a kitten could get tangled up in. Look for small things lying around that could be chewed or swallowed, for example, coins, hair-clips, pen lids, guitar picks, etc. Basically, look for anything that you would not let a small child play with.

You may need to reconsider where certain items live and find new homes for them, like in cupboards or on higher shelves. You might need to consider replacing open bins and waste paper baskets with closed-top ones.

You should pay special attention to wires and electrical cords. We have multiple gadgets and devices in our lives these days, and our homes are filled with all kinds of phone chargers and laptop cables, and electrical cords. You might need to consolidate some of these into a neater arrangement and use cable organizers or cable boxes.

Initially, your sweet little kitten will be sticking to the floor or low-set furniture like the sofa. So the things you have on your dressing table or around the bathroom sink should be okay for now. But by about 6 months of age, kitten will have grown sufficiently to jump up onto most surfaces around the home. At that point, you will *have* to look at how you store all those various perfumes and lotions and creams that you don't want the cat getting into, so it might be worth looking at that now anyway. Cats often delight themselves in being able to knock items off a surface with their paws, and you don't want to come home to find your expensive bottle of perfume smashed on the bathroom floor.

Recliner Chairs

The humble recliner chair is not something obvious that you would immediately think of as dangerous. After all, it is something that makes your life easier and more pleasurable. But this luxurious item that is bringing comfort and ease to *your* life is a whole world of danger for your kitten!

Cats love to get underneath things and into tight spaces, and you will always find them crawling out from underneath furniture. So if you are not aware that your kitten is sleeping under your chair when you operate the recliner mechanism, it could have very dire and tragic consequences.

If you have a recliner, the one simple rule is: make sure you KNOW the whereabouts of your kitten before operating it, either up or down.

So my advice is that it's best to moderate your use of your recliner for a little while, at least until you get used to having a cat around.

If you have an Electric Recliner, I recommend unplugging it from the power outlet for a while so that you don't operate it absent-mindedly, at least until you get used to sharing your home with a pet. Or, if you have a Manual Recliner, try taping a piece of cardboard onto the handle to act as a reminder whenever you go to operate it without thinking. That way, you are going to keep Kitten safe, and at the same time, train yourself to always be aware of the cat before reclining into your favorite position.

Once you have got used to having a cat around all the time, you can plug your Electric Recliner back into the power outlet, but still take it easy and stay aware.

Houseplants

Something you definitely need to check is the types of plants you have in your home. Why? Well, because some plants are poisonous to cats, especially Lilies.

Any plant in the Lily family can cause problems, but some are worse than others. Easter Lily, Tiger Lily, and Stargazer Lily can cause kidney failure if a cat eats any part of the plant. So you need to make sure that you remove any Lilies or any plants you suspect might be Lilies.

If your cat is allowed outside, you should also check your garden and make sure you remove any Lilies from there too. In the long term, you also need to make sure that any flower arrangements you bring into the home do not contain Lilies.

Note, if your cat does get exposed to Lily poisoning, you cannot treat them at home. You will need to take them to a vet as soon as possible.

Where to keep your cat

Once your new cutie has settled-in as part of the family, they will most likely have the run of the house, but that is a few weeks away yet.

When they first come to your home, you will want to restrict them to a smaller portion of the premises, if you can, so that they are not overwhelmed as they try and get used to a new environment. So, depending on the layout of your home, you should consider whether you have an area that can be closed off from the rest of the house for a little while.

I am not talking about just one small room, like a utility room, but rather a couple of rooms or a small section of the home. For example, if you have a living area that can be closed off from the bedrooms by closing a door or two, that would be ideal.

You should also be looking at whether that area can be closed off at night, even after they have settled in. That way, they can occupy the whole house during the day but be restricted to that smaller area whilst you are asleep. This is because you don't really want your small kitten running about the hallway and bedroom area when you get up to go to the bathroom in the middle of the night. You could be at risk of treading on them or mistakenly shutting them into the bathroom or your bedroom without realizing it.

Where to put everything

There are three things you need to consider the placement of carefully: (i) the feeding bowls, (ii) the litter tray, and (iii) the cat bed.

If you have identified an area that can be closed off for them at night, you need to place all three of those items within that area because you don't want to shut-off access to their bowls or litter tray at night.

You also need to think about whether the initial placement is where you plan to keep each item in the long term. Once your kitten has got used to where things live, you don't want to confuse them by regularly moving things around. If you keep moving the litter tray, for example, they may get confused as to where they need to do their business, with unfortunate results! So try and keep things in the same place if at all possible.

If you do have to move it, try not to do it too often, and make sure you take the time to show your kitten where it has moved to.

Bed

Ideally, the bed should be tucked away somewhere cozy, like under a coffee table against a wall; or in a corner down behind the TV. Your cat will probably not use it all that much, preferring to sleep on your sofa or favorite armchair during the daytime. But when they do want to get away from it all, they need to feel like they have a cozy, safe place to retreat to. So if you can make it feel like the bed is in a dark little cave, they will love it and be more likely to use it.

Bowls

The food and water bowls should be placed on the opposite side of the room to the litter tray (because none of us like to poop where we eat!). You want to make sure that they are out of the line of foot traffic so that no-one is accidentally knocking the cat as they walk past when they are trying to eat. If the area is carpeted, you would be wise to put down some kind of tray or mat to place the bowls on. That would help define the feeding area and also catch any spills of food and water, keeping them off your lovely, clean carpet.

Litter tray

The litter tray should be placed in a corner, rather than along the middle of a wall. It needs to feel like a secure, safe place so that the cat doesn't feel vulnerable and develop any anxiety issues about using the litter.

When your cat uses the tray, they will cover-over their business with the loose fresh litter by flicking it up with their paws. So having it surrounded by two walls also helps inhibit the spread of any litter that gets accidentally kicked out of the tray as they do so.

You should set-up the litter tray before you first bring your kitten home, as this will be the first place you show them when they arrive. Put a fresh liner in, and fill the tray to a depth of about an inch and a half, or roughly

3cm to 4cm. Your kitten will be used to using litter by this age and will instinctively know what to do with it.

The indoor or outdoor question

One of the things you need to decide before you bring your cat home is whether you are going to allow them to go outside or whether you want them to live indoors full-time.

If you have never owned a cat before, you might not realize is that they are not always calm, docile animals that lounge around all day like Garfield. They are natural hunters in the wild and have a hunting instinct even when they are hand-fed and live indoors in a soft-furnished home. So there are certain times each day when your calm, peaceful kitten will turn into a madman.

The hunting instinct will kick in; their eyes will go big, their ears will stick up, and off they go, tearing around the house in a frenzy, like kids on a sugar rush. Running from room to room, leaping onto the furniture, they race around, just wanting to get all their energy out in one quick burst. Then 10 mins later, they are back to the usual cat's life of sleeping, watching TV, and sleeping some more. This behavior can be a little surprising if you are not expecting it, but it is all part of the feline charm.

So deciding whether you want to allow them out of the house for that hunting playtime is a crucial decision to be made up-front. Once you take the cat home, it has to be either allowed free access to roam outside or be trained to stay indoors all the time. You can't go back and forth between the two

Neither way is right or wrong; it is simply your choice. Personally, I like to keep cats inside, but that is just my preference. Overall, you need to consider what will work best for you in your circumstance and what availability you will have to look after your cat. At the end of the day, if you have small children running in and out of the house into the backyard all day, there might be little chance of getting your cat to stay in all the time.

When cats are allowed to roam freely outside, however, they are more at risk, being exposed to the possibility of worms, ticks, and fleas, and also to poisonous plants. Outdoor cats are more likely to get into "hissing" fights with other cats, and tiny kittens can also be at risk from natural predators such as foxes and birds of prey.

However, always remember that the main danger to any cat is of human origin: - the dreaded automobile! You can't teach a cat how to cross a road safely using a pedestrian crossing, so they are always at risk of getting hit by a car. If you do allow them outside, you might find it desirable to invest in some kind of pet insurance to help cover vet bills, if needed.

One more thing to be aware of is the situation with the local by-laws where you live. Some local councils have rules about not letting cats out at night since they see them as feral pests that hunt and kill the local native fauna. Most counties will have some kind of pet registration procedure, but some may also have a curfew requiring cats to be kept indoors after a particular time in the evening.

So make sure you check to see if your local council has a cat curfew or other rules about letting cats roam free. You may have to make sure that your cat is indoors at night.

Once you are sure that you have got everything ready, it is time to bring your cat home. Let the kitten-parenting begin!

Chapter 6

Introducing Kitten to Your Home

"I had been told that the training procedure with cats was difficult. It's not. Mine had me trained in two days."

Bill Dana

WHAT A GREAT DAY, your kitten is coming home!

Picking up your kitten, putting them in the car, and bringing them home is so exciting, ...but in all that excitement, don't forget to take your new pet carrier with you! It's easily done. If you do forget your pet carrier, I suggest going back home again to fetch it. Don't risk driving Kitten home without adequate protection.

Picking them up

When you get there, try and spend a few minutes playing with your new kitten to bond with them. Let them sniff your hand and get to know you by your scent. Try gently stroking them on the top of their skull and the side of their cheek with the back of your hand. When kittens greet each other, they rub the tops of their heads together as a way of saying "Hello," and using the back of your hand mimics that action. Despite your excitement, treat them gently so that they know you are a safe person to be around.

If you are not used to holding a cat, you need to pick them up carefully by placing one hand under the chest and then putting your other hand or arm under their feet to support them. Try not to pick them up by putting your hand under their belly as that may hurt them, and they might try to jump out of your grip. Spend a few minutes playing with them and acquainting yourself with them.

When you are ready to leave, pick them up and place them gently into the pet carrier and close the door, making sure that the clasp is properly secured. You shouldn't have to wrestle with them to get them in the carrier, kittens are naturally inquisitive, but they may want to have a good sniff of it first before you pop them in.

You will naturally want to carry them gently as you head towards your car, but don't be scared and handle the carrier *too* gently, as any the cat may sense your uneasiness if you are too anxious. Place the pet carrier onto the car seat next to you, the rear seat is best, and have someone else drive so that you can hold on to the carrier and reassure your kitten during the journey.

Getting home

Once you reach home, you want to take the pet carrier through to that part of the house you have decided that

Kitten will live in. You should put the carrier down on the floor somewhere near the litter tray and open the carrier door. Then wait. Let kitten come out of the carrier in her own time. She will want to explore very gradually at first.

Entering a new environment can be a stressful thing for a kitten, so you will need to take things gently. Your home is a place they have never been before, and there are no smells that they recognize to make them feel at ease. Cats are scent-based creatures; they recognize people, places, and things by their smell. So your kitten will want to explore with her nose. She will sniff the carpet before walking on it; she will sniff the furniture before touching it; she will sniff the litter box before using it. She will sniff everything.

Once she has come out of the pet carrier and is gingerly sniffing around her, pick her up, and gently place her in the litter tray. Move her front paws around in it a little so that she knows it is loose litter. She may have been a little anxious on the journey and may need to use it straight away. Or she might just want to sniff it and scratch around a little, then climb out to start exploring other things. But by showing her the litter straight away, you are training her early on as to where she can relieve herself when she needs to.

In those first 10 mins or so, she may not get very far, possibly staying within a few feet of the pet carrier. She may even want to go back into the pet carrier for a while. If she does, don't fret; just leave her be. Stand back and give her some space. She will start exploring when she is ready. It might be best for you to go and sit down on the sofa and watch her from across the room. Let her gain confidence in her new surroundings in her own time.

As she gently moves around, you will notice that she is sniffing literally everything she comes across. As she does so, she is "mapping" out the room and committing it to memory as an odor map so that she can recognize where she is later on.

Eventually, she will come over to you and start sniffing you. When she does, you can stroke her and pick her up and cuddle her. But then put her down again to continue exploring. Show her where the food and water bowls are, ensuring that you have already filled the water bowl.

After she has been home for about twenty or thirty minutes, you should put out a small amount of dry food so that she can nibble if she wants to. The purpose of putting some food out now is not really to feed her; but rather to help calm her fears about her new environment and show her that all of her needs will be taken care of here. If you have shown her that there is food here, water here, and somewhere to relieve herself here; she can relax and feel start to feel at home.

Once your kitten has explored for a little while, all that excitement may have tired her out, and she may want to find a quiet place to sleep for a while. She might disappear under some furniture or find a dark corner, but she may also go back into the pet carrier if you have left it on the floor. Let her do that, as it is obviously somewhere she trusts and feels safe in.

Remember that just like babies, young kittens will want to sleep often. Their day will seem like one long sleep, punctuated by short periods of being awake. But that will gradually change as they grow, and their awake periods become longer.

When she wakes up, try to resist the urge to over-cuddle her. Give her plenty of space and let her keep exploring at her own pace, but make sure you put her onto the litter again to remind her where it is.

Feeding

Once it gets toward the early evening, it is time to give Kitten her first proper meal. As mentioned earlier, you should start by giving your kitten the same food that she was eating at the breeder or pet shop. She is experiencing enough changes as it is, without having to deal with a new diet, so try and keep the type of food, the amounts, and the routine the same as she is used to, for the time being.

Most likely, that will mean serving a small amount of meat, probably 20g to 30g, twice a day, with a little bit of dry food mixed into it so that she gets used to eating both types of food. That should be set out in her bowl at the same time each morning and evening so that you establish a routine. Show her where it is when you do. You should leave it out for about half an hour or so, certainly not more than an hour, then take it away. She may have a few attempts at eating it during that time, but once the time is up, take it away even if she hasn't finished it. That way, you will train her to eat at those specific times, and you won't be leaving meat out for long periods to go rotten. When you take it away, you should put some dry food out in her grazing bowl that she can nibble on in-between mealtimes.

Food

The dry food you give your kitten should be specifically labeled as a "Complete Kitten food," as this will have all the minerals and nutrients they need while their bodies are growing so rapidly. They should eat Kitten food for the full first twelve months; after that, you can change to an Adult cat variety, which will have a different composition to support optimal health in adult cats.

For wet food, I like to give them a good quality tinned all-meat product. There are cheaper ones at the grocery store, but I prefer to use quality food, with no "filler." Wet food is important because it contains moisture and ensures that your kitten is getting enough water into their bodies. You *can* just feed them dry kitten food if you want, but you will have to make sure they drink water regularly to maintain hydration.

The cans of food I use contain about five meals worth for a kitten, so I keep the unused portion in the fridge, in the can with a re-usable tin lid on it. When I use the cold meat from the refrigerator, I like to give the bowl a few seconds in the microwave before setting it down. Six to eight seconds in the microwave is plenty: just enough to take the chill off, but not enough to make the food hot. This is because if the food is too cold, it will not produce an aroma, and it is the aroma that is appealing and makes your cat want to eat. So. if your cat is being fussy and not eating, try warming their food for just a few seconds in the microwave to make it more appetizing.

Many canned cat foods contain fish, so you would assume that all cats love to eat fish, but this is not really the case. Certain breeds do not like fish very much at all; and some cats are put off by the smell of it in the house. But even cats that *do* like fish should not be fed fish exclusively; they should be fed a varied diet that includes other meats as well.

I also avoid all the special "gourmet-with-gravy" types of cat food commonly found in grocery stores these days. After all, cats are not humans, and these meals are being marketed to appeal to our human tastes to make us buy them, rather than being something that will actually appeal to a cat's simple feline dietary requirements. I prefer to but cat food based on the nutritional value and quality of ingredients rather than the gourmet appeal.

The first week

As mentioned in the previous chapter, for the first five or six days or so, it is best to keep your kitten to a restricted, smaller part of the house, if you can.

Even though she will have the full run of the house eventually, keeping her in a smaller area for a while will allow her to settle in and get used to living with you without being overwhelmed with too much new experience all at once. It also saves more fun for later when you gradually introduce her to other parts of the house. Each new room she is allowed into will become a grand adventure in itself.

But for now, try and keep her relatively contained. Remember, she is a small *baby* animal, and you need to create a "nursery" type of environment for her as the introductory experience to your world.

Your cat may seem shy for those first few days as she gradually gets comfortable and familiarises herself with everything. So for the first week, you want to take it easy. It's probably best NOT to invite all your friends and family over to see your kitten in the first few days. Wait seven to ten days before entertaining visitors.

For that first week or so, your kitten will still be getting used to the new environment she finds herself in. She needs to be given a chance to acclimatize herself and get accustomed to living in your home, as well as getting used to living with you! Having extra people around could overwhelm her and cause anxiety, so it's better to wait until you and your kitten have bonded and she seems confident in her new surroundings. Then you can invite your family over to "Ooh!" and "Aah!" and congratulate you on acquiring such a beautiful new companion!

Chapter 7

Understanding your cat's behavior

"I have lived with several Zen Masters – all of them cats."

Eckhart Tolle

YOUR FIRST FEW WEEKS with a new kitten are so wonderful as you spend time getting to know them and learn all about their personality and behavior.

If this is your first cat, though, you may not yet understand cat behavior and what it means. There may be a few surprising cat behaviors that seem strange if you have never come across them before.

Despite their reputation for finding a quiet spot to keep away-from-it-all and sleep away the day, when they are awake, they love to get involved and interact with you. Whether they are brushing against you, licking you, staring at you, biting you, sitting on your laptop, or stealing your favorite seat, they are just trying to let you know that they love you and feel happy when you are around.

Playing

Cats love to play. Kitten play is all based around their most natural activity: hunting. When they play, all their favorite moves are hunting practice. Running around like crazy, jumping on the furniture, darting out from under cover, attacking objects, and sitting low to the floor before pouncing are all moves from the feline hunting playbook.

When you want Kitten to have some fun, just grab a cat wand toy and jingle the bell. Your cat will immediately get into hunting mode and get in the crouched position to start pouncing. They will delight as you move the object around for them to attack it as if it were a small mouse-like creature. This is such an innate behavior for them, and they need to engage in it daily.

How to tell when your cat is happy

When a cat is happy with you, it lets you know it. When it seeks your attention, it is showing that it likes you and wants to interact with you. If it didn't feel happy with you, it would avoid you, so whenever your cat comes to you and tries to get your attention, you know you are onto a good thing.

When a cat walks between your feet, brushing up against your legs, it is acknowledging that you are one of their family and claiming affinity with you. They have pheromone glands in their cheeks, and when they rub their check on you, they are marking you with their smell to say that "this one is part of my gang."

Purring

When a cat is purring, you know that it is content. The purring sound is made by moving the diaphragm to push air up through the throat in such a way as to make the larynx vibrate. Purring seems to be a relaxation behavior that cats exhibit when they are feeling secure and safe. The sound is also relaxing and reassuring for us humans. However, some more recent research indicates that cats may also purr when they are upset or scared and need to calm themselves down and "find a happy place."[5]

Tail waving

Everyone knows that a dog that is wagging its tail is a happy dog, right? Well, a cat also indicates its mood with its tail.

When your cat approaches you with its tail straight up in the air and curled over at the end like a shepherds crook, it is telling you that it is happy and wants to interact with you. The same is true when it is swishing the end of its tail gently from side to side. It will also do this when it is focused on playing with a toy and getting ready to pounce on it playfully.

However, when it is flicking its whole tail quickly from side to side, beware! It is an indication that your cat is irritated or annoyed.

Body Language

There is a lot you can tell about how your cat is feeling just by looking at their posture. There are some generalities to the meaning of a cat's body positions, but each cat does have its own unique personality, so not all body language is going to mean the same thing for all cats. So get to know your kitten well, and you will be able to tell their mood by how they are sitting or lying.

Belly Up - When a cat rolls onto its back and lies there with its belly exposed, it is a sign that they are feeling relaxed and safe in their environment. You may find that your cat greets you when you come home by rolling around on their back in front of you with their belly exposed. This is an indication that they are glad to see you and feeling happy and relaxed now that you are here.

They will want some attention from you. However, even though their belly is exposed, they are NOT asking for a belly rub! Dogs may love having their belly rubbed, but cats don't. If you try, you will immediately find claws and teeth gripping onto your hand. The relaxed belly-up pose may be a sign of trust, but your cat doesn't want you to taking advantage of that trust.

Crouched – When a cat sits crouched low to the floor with their feet tucked underneath them, it can mean one of two things. If they look alert, they may be in hunting mode, getting ready to pounce. But if they look timid and eyes closed, it may be that they are feeling a little anxious and scared. By putting their feet under them, they are trying to make themselves look as small as possible and avoid the world.

Sleeping Croissant – the classic sleeping position of a cat is with its tail and hind legs pulled round to meet its front legs and head, in a croissant or crescent moon shape. This is an indication that your cat is feeling very safe and secure, and they will sleep soundly in this position. Having their body curled up helps them preserve their body heat and lets them sleep deeply for a long time.

Sleeping stretched out – when your cat sleeps on their side with their arms stretched out in front of their head, they will usually also have their eyes half-open. This indicates they are trying to take a nap but are trying to stay partially alert for danger. They can easily wake and move quickly from this position.

Farmhouse Loaf – when a cat is lying on its stomach with its legs under its body and arms placed in front of it, in a neat, formal pose, it looks a bit like a tall loaf of bread. Its eyes may be closed, but it is not fully asleep; it is just resting with its eyes closed. This position means that the cat is content and happy just to sit there. My cat often sits like this, basking in the warmth of the sunlight coming in through the window.

Other strange behaviors

Kneading

One of the strangest behaviors that new cat owners are surprised by is a behavior known as "kneading" or "kneading biscuits." This is something that came as a surprise to me, as I certainly had never heard of this before we had our second cat; and our first cat never did it.

"Kneading" is when you find your cat pushing down on a soft object, like a cushion or blanket, with their front paws and moving them back and forth in a rhythmic motion. It looks for all the world as if they are "kneading" some dough, ready to bake some bread or make a batch of cookies. They will usually be sitting up as they do so, but with a younger kitten, you may find they also have their face down "suckling" on the blanket as they knead.

This strange behavior is just your cat regressing to their early childhood, reliving the days of their younger selves when they were part of a litter, nursing on their mother. You will usually find that they are lightly purring while they do this and that they might fall off to sleep afterward.

It is the cat equivalent of a human child sucking their thumb, reminding themselves of the comfort of breastfeeding. The suckling action is easy to understand, but why the kneading? Well, when a kitten is breastfeeding, it uses its front paws to gently massage its mother's tummy to encourage the milk to flow freely. That action reminds them of nursing as much as the suckling does.

When your cat is kneading, it indicates that they are feeling very safe, secure, and content and are demonstrating that by settling down for a cozy relaxation session. If your cat comes and sits on you and starts purring and kneading in your lap, you should feel honored that they feel so relaxed and comfortable with you. They are letting you know that you make them feel as safe and secure as they did with their own mother. What a compliment!

Slow blinking

Another way that your kitten will communicate their love and acceptance of you is through blinking. When your soft bundle of fur sits quietly in front of you and stares at you with those big yellow eyes and either squints at you through half-closed eyes or slowly opens and closes their eyelids, you know you are in their good books. This is the cat equivalent of human kisses. You can usually "feel" their approval of you at those times, as it is quite a special, intimate moment between you and your beloved feline.

Seat stealing

You will often find that when you get up out of your seat for a couple of minutes to go to the bathroom or put the kettle on, your cat is sitting in your chair when you return. When a cat steals your seat, it is just another way they are acknowledging that they feel connected to you and part of the same family unit. When you get up, you vacate a spot that is both warm and full of your scent. Since they love you, and they love warmth, they move straight into that spot. And they are always reluctant to give it up when you return.

Keyboard walking

Another common cat behavior that can sometimes be annoying is a cat's propensity to walk across your computer keyboard as you are trying to type.

Whether you at your desk trying to get that report finished or sitting on the sofa doing some online shopping with your laptop, it seems that your cat knows how to interrupt you in the most inconvenient way. One minute you are typing away with proficiency, and the next minute your cat is literally sitting on your hands.

Why is that? Can they not see that we are busy and don't want to be interrupted? Do they not know that we don't want a whole string of percentage signs typed across the screen?

Well, of course, they have absolutely no idea about what we are doing with the computer; they just know that our hands are there, and our hands are moving. And if our hands are moving, they want to get in on the action and have those hands moving on them to stroke and caress them. It is quite smart on their part!

Bringing Gifts

As part of their natural hunting behavior, cats like to "catch" things and bring them to you, proud of their "kill." My cat likes to bring me tissues. She pulls a tissue from a Kleenex box somewhere around the house, chews it up a bit, and carries it in her mouth to the kitchen. She drops it on the kitchen floor and emits a particular "Meow" that she only uses for that purpose. That Meow says: "Here, I have caught something, and I have brought it to the kitchen for you because I know that is where you prepare the food."

Your cat might find some other type of object to bring you, but it will always find some way to contribute. If your cat is allowed outside and it happens to catch a bird or a mouse, it will bring it into where you prepare the food. It is just their way of trying to share the burden of supplying the food.

Boxes

Most cats love crawling under things and getting into tight spaces, but some cats seem to make it an art form. To that effect, you may find that your cat loves getting into cardboard boxes.

Some cats just love boxes: big boxes, small boxes, short boxes, long boxes – most cats are box-crazy! No sooner have you unpacked your latest online-shopping purchase that just arrived in the mail, when you look down and notice that your cat has already climbed in to the empty box! You often find them head-deep, with their backside sticking out as they try to squeeze into even the tiniest of boxes that they will never fit into!

As you get to know your cat you will discover other interesting things about them. In many ways, they are very much like humans: each cat has their own unique personality and quirks. Some are playful, some are gentle. Some are fussy, some are bossy. Some are stoic and serene, others are whimsical. Whatever personality your cat has, one thing is for sure – they will always love their owner!

Chapter 8

General Care and Training

"The way to get on with a cat is to treat it as an equal – or even better, as the superior it knows itself to be."

Elizabeth Peters

NOW THAT YOUR CAT IS HOME and getting used to being part of your family, you need to know how to properly look after them and ensure they integrate smoothly into the routine of your family life.

The good news is that love cats love routine and will appreciate things operating the same way each day.

Making sure that mealtimes are regular helps them settle and feel secure. If things do go a little out of whack with your routine, it can cause upset, which can lead to behavioral problems if the cat starts to feel anxious. So it important to monitor your cat's mood and make sure they seem content and are coping well with life in your household.

Despite that, cats are generally very easy to take care of and require minimal maintenance. But there are a few things you need to do in taking care of your cat and a few things to monitor and take corrective action over if they go awry.

Litter training

Cats will automatically use a litter tray as an instinctive behavior from when they are very small kittens. The pet shop or breeder will have made sure that they got used to doing so, and in general, you shouldn't have any problems.

Nevertheless, make sure your cat knows where the litter tray is as soon as you introduce them to your home. Then, for the first week or so, make a point of placing them onto the litter tray every now and then, especially after they wake from a long nap.

Praise them whenever you see them using the litter to reinforce the use of the tray as the *only place* to do their business. Make sure you remove any solids as soon as they are dry and clean the tray of wet clumps daily so that the tray does not start to smell: the last thing you want is for the tray to become smelly and off-putting for a kitten to use.

If you have a large house, you may want to consider having more than one litter tray placed around the home so that the litter is more accessible and convenient to find. If you have a house with two or more floors, you should have one tray upstairs and one downstairs, at a minimum. Try to keep the trays in set places, though, not moving them around all the time. If the kitten starts getting confused about the location of the litter, you could be asking for problems.

Correcting Litter Tray issues if they develop

If your kitten does have an accident outside of the tray, be careful not to get angry or punish them. They are not likely to relate your punishment directly to their toilet mistake, and your anger could stress them and exacerbate the problem. Instead, just clean the area well with water and white vinegar so that the smell is removed, and keep encouraging them in the correct use of the tray.

If you find them regularly going outside of the tray, the first thing to try is to change the type of litter. Cats can be fussy, and if the feel or smell of one kind of litter is not to their preference, they might refuse to use it. If you suspect that is the case, just try another kind. The absorbent-crystal type, for example, is loved by some cats because it soaks up the urine very well, but other cats find it too rough and sharp on their paws.

If changing the litter does not remedy the issue, or if your cat suddenly stops using the litter after a long period of no problem with it, then it is best to schedule a check-up with the vet. Inappropriate urination can be caused by a urinary tract infection or other medical issue, and inappropriate defecation can be brought on by stress or anxiety. Have a think about whether there is anything happening at home that may be causing them anxiety. Are there loud noises in the home? Are your kids harassing the kitten in any way? Are you cleaning the litter regularly? Is the litter tray in what the cat may perceive as an unsafe area? e.g., in a place where everyone in the family is walking past all the time? Moving it to a quieter area might solve the issue.

Trimming claws

Claw trimming is an essential cat-care task, especially if you have children. After all, you don't want your little ones heading off to school with big cat-scratch marks up their arms.

Some people get scared of having to trim cat claws, but it is an easy task really, and it gets easier the more you do it. Start trimming regularly when your kitten is young, and they will get used to it very quickly. You will find that they need clipping roughly every two weeks.

The primary skill to use when trimming claws is "confidence." If you try and trim claws while feeling nervous and apologetic, the kitten will resist and try and wriggle out of your arms. But if you hold them firmly but gently and let them know that you are in charge, they will relax and let you do it. It is best to choose a quieter time, though, don't try and do it when they are all playful and energetic because they will not want to sit still for you.

The best method is to sit them on a table in front of you, holding them between your arms but against your body, so that they are facing away from you. Then use one hand to take hold of a paw and gently squeeze the paw to expose one claw at a time. Simply slip the nail clippers over the curved white portion of the claw and clip it. When you look closely, you will see a darker core in the middle of the claw. Be careful to only clip the white part, and stay well away from the darker part. Cat claws are just like human fingernails: if you clip only the white part, you are fine, but if you cut too close to the quick, they can bleed. If you do happen to clip the darker part and cause bleeding, don't worry; just dab with a tissue, and it will stop in a few minutes.

Failing that, if you find you are just unable to get them to sit still and submit to being clipped, there are two other options open to you:

1. Get the vet to clip their claws for you. This may seem the easiest because you don't have to do it yourself, but it does mean all the hassle of having to book-in an appointment, get the cat to the vet, etc. Most vets will be all too happy to clip your cat's claws for free as part of a scheduled visit for a check-up or some other issue, but if you are booking an appointment just to get claws clipped they may charge a fee.

2. The other easy option is to try and clip your kitten's claws while they are asleep. If your cat likes to fall asleep on your lap in the evenings, this could work out well for you. Just keep the clippers close to your armchair, and choose your timing well. The cat needs to be in that zoned-out, deep

sleep stage of their nap. If they are not deeply asleep, you are likely to wake them by clipping. Even though they are sleeping, try and maneuver them gently to get access to their paws without being too rough and waking them.

Brushing

As previously mentioned, cats are naturally self-cleaning creatures that love to groom themselves and keep themselves meticulously clean. On a day-to-day basis, they will lick their coat to remove dirt and any loose hairs. They seem to do a pretty good job of it all by themselves, but they appreciate any help you can give them by brushing them regularly. Brushing your kitten is something you should start in the first few days so that they get used to it from an early age.

When you brush your cat, do it gently as if you are petting and stroking them. They will be very inquisitive about the brush at first and will want to sniff it and probably bite it before they let you use it on them. Let them. Let them get familiar with it so that they trust it when you bring it near them.

Start at the top of the head between their ears, and brush smoothly down along their back. They may not like it at first and keep trying to turn around and grab the brush, but that is okay. Once they get used to gentle strokes down the head and along the back, they may let you brush their sides and even their tail as well. As they get more familiar with brushing, they will come to enjoy it and enjoy the interaction with you. However, they will need to get very comfortable with the whole process before they let you get the brush anywhere near their tummy.

Your cat will need more brushing at the start of summer because they will molt and shed hair to have a lighter, cooler coat for the warmer months.

Hairballs

When cats lick themselves, the loose hairs get swallowed and should pass through the digestive tract with no problems. However, if your cat swallows a lot of hair, they may have difficulty digesting all of it, and it can accumulate in the stomach as a hairball.

Cats usually don't get problems with hairballs when they are a kitten because their hair is shorter and thinner. But when they are adults, their hair is thicker and harder to digest. Also, longer-haired breeds are more likely to swallow much more of it and require brushing far more often to prevent hairballs.

When a cat does develop a hairball, it deals with it by vomiting it up. This may come as a shock the first time you see it. Your cat will start making strange noises and start convulsing their body as they retch and try to eject the hairball. Don't be alarmed; it's a natural process: they might look like they are in distress, but they are not. Once they get it up, don't scold them, even though you now have a small icky mess to clean up with a piece of paper towel. Instead, congratulate them and praise them for doing a good job!

Bathing

You don't need to bathe your cat unless they accidentally get covered in something that will be too much of a cleaning job for them to handle themselves. For example, if they go outside, they might get covered in mud, which they cannot lick off by themselves. Or even inside the home, they might manage to get covered in something that needs to be washed off, especially if you have younger children that like to play with them (tomato sauce on a cat, anyone?)

Bathing a cat is relatively simple but is not something they would naturally enjoy. So you just need to keep them calm and keep reassuring them throughout the procedure so that they don't freak out and try and jump out halfway through, scratching you in the process.

What you need:

1. Sink, or bath, or large bucket – a plastic baby bath is ideal

2. Cat shampoo – not human shampoo, which could irritate them

3. Towel – a good size to wrap them up in afterward

4. Face Washer or washcloth

5. Plastic jug - for rinsing them

Method:

Fill the bath or sink with warm water, not too deep and not too hot. Just deep enough to cover their legs if they were standing, and just warm enough to feel inviting and relaxing, without any risk of feeling too hot and make them want to jump out. Just like a baby's bathwater, test the temperature with your elbow.

1. Gradually lower the cat into the water, letting them get used to it until they are sitting in it, being held gently, but firmly, by you.

2. Use the jug to gently pour water over their body to wet all their fur, but avoid pouring any on their head, face, or ears.

3. Squirt a small amount of cat shampoo on to them and massage into their fur to produce a soapy lather. Work your way all over their coat, being careful with sensitive areas.

4. Then rinse off with more water from the jug, being careful to remove all the suds so that they are not left licking shampoo off themselves later on. You might want to have a spare bucket of clean, lukewarm water on hand to rinse with so that you are not just rinsing the shampoo back onto them from the water they are sitting in.

5. Wet the face washer and squeeze it out before using it to clean the face, head, and ears gently. Be careful, as their whiskers are very sensitive, and they may not like you touching them.

6. Once Kitten is clean, you can lift them out of the water onto a nice big clean towel on your lap. They will love being wrapped up in a towel after a bath, just like you do. Make a fuss of them while you towel them off, and let them know how good they have been. Getting them towel-dry should be

enough. As long as they don't feel too wet, they should be okay to finish the drying process naturally themselves. Remember, cats in the wild get wet in the rain and manage to dry off okay, all by themselves.

Afterward, let them wander off and find a quiet place to relax and recover from the ordeal. For most cats, having a bath is a two-edged sword: on the one hand they don't like the experience of being wet, but on the other hand, they love all the attention and fuss they get from you. But they will probably still want to go and get some "alone time" to reflect on the experience.

Behavioral issues and how to handle them

Sometimes, Kitten will do what you consider the wrong thing; but to them, they are just doing what comes naturally. So when they don't follow your house rules, you need to train them how you want them to behave.

The best way is to avoid telling them off or getting angry with them and instead just pointing their behavior in the right direction. Discourage wrong behavior by steering them away from it, and encourage correct behavior by praising them for doing the right thing.

Biting

Kittens are always born as part of a litter and naturally, love interacting and playing with others. So they are times they will want to roll around and wrestle with you as if you are one of their siblings.

Using their mouth to grab hold of you is a natural part of that interaction. A cat will not be trying to bite you to hurt you; they will just be using one of the few assets they have to interact with you. But it is something you want to discourage so that they don't hurt you or your children as they play. So if they start biting, just simply put pull your hand away or set them down on the floor. That takes the fun out of it for them and communicates that this not a way you want them to behave with you. They soon get the idea.

Climbing curtains

Cats are natural climbing creatures. In the wild, they climb trees or other structures and love getting up high. It gives them a safe place to view their surroundings and look out for prey to catch. But it's not so great when that natural climbing instinct kicks-in as they sit in on your lounge room floor, staring up at your beautiful new velvet drapes!

There are several ways to prevent them from climbing drapes or curtains or even insect-screen doors. Try and block off direct access by putting something on the floor in front of the curtains. This makes it harder for the cat to sit directly in front of them, thereby reducing the temptation. Some people advise putting some aluminum kitchen foil down on the floor in front of the curtains because cats hate the feeling of walking on it.

If your cat does start climbing your curtains, don't get angry with them; just gently pick them up and put them out of the room for a few minutes. If they do it again, remove them again. Repeat that as many times as you need to until they start to lose interest in the curtains. The only danger here is that they begin to associate the bad behavior with getting attention. To counteract this, make the time-out a little longer each time, and they will gradually lose interest.

If you ever see your cat sitting there, looking up at the curtain ready to climb, but then change their mind and walk away, make sure you praise them for resisting the urge.

Whatever tactic you use, remember that it is only a temporary measure that you need to use for a few days or weeks to train them out of making inappropriate climbing a habit. Once they have got the idea, they tend to stick with it. If they try climbing again a few months later, simply repeat the process to reinforce the correct behavior again.

Climbing on restricted tables or furniture

There will be certain pieces of furniture or places you don't want your cat climbing onto. For example, the kitchen bench-top where you prepare your food is an obvious one. Again, the process here is one of discouraging wrong behavior and praising correct behavior until the correct behavior sticks.

There are also some practical steps you can take, like moving any nearby lower furniture that might serve as a stepping stone for Kitten to reach the high kitchen bench. If they learn not to go there while they are small, they will generally not attempt to go there when they are bigger and able to leap up in one bound.

Remember that it is a natural thing for cats to want to climb, so its good if can provide them some other way of doing so that you approve of. Having some kind of cat scratcher climbing-tree in your home is a great way to allow them to climb without damaging any of your lovely furnishings and will give them an elevated perch from which to view their world.

Chapter 9

Healthcare

"The only thing a cat worries about is what's happening right now."
Lloyd Alexander

ONCE YOU OWN A PET, you want to keep them healthy, and the best way to do that is by regular visits to the vet.

You should arrange a first health-check appointment with a vet within the first two to three days of bringing your kitten home. This is to make sure that the cat you have been sold does not have any health issues and has a clean bill of health. Whatever claims the shop or breeder may have made about the cat's condition can only be verified by getting them checked by a professional.

If you buy your cat from a decent-sized pet shop, they will often have an arrangement with a local vet for a free check-up as part of your purchase. This is a good arrangement for both the pet shop and the vet, as it ensures that they both have continued business.

I would certainly take up that free appointment. However, you are not obliged to use the vet that the pet shop recommends; you can go to any vet you like, though you will be paying for that check-up unless your chosen alternative vet has a "free first-appointment" offer.

At your appointment, the vet will examine your cat and check for all the common health issues. If they happened to find a significant problem like a genetic disease or some other serious illness, you should be able to take the animal back to the pet shop or breeder and get your money back. However, there is usually only a seven day limit on that warranty, which is why it is so essential to get the health check done in the first few days.

The vet will talk to you about worming and flea treatments, which are the two essential home medications that your cat will require, and also about continuing their course of vaccinations, which will have already been started before you became the owner. They should also explain to you about de-sexing, which, as a first-time cat owner, is something you should definitely get done.

Medications

Your kitten will require a couple of medications on an ongoing basis to keep them in the best of health:

Worm Tablets

Like most four-legged pets, cats are susceptible to getting worms. Tape-worm, Lung-worm, and Heart-worm are all possible afflictions for cats, so it is essential to give them worm tablets.

A kitten should be given a worm treatment once a month for the first six months, then three-monthly after that, though you will need to check the instructions on the worming product you buy, as they may differ. You will usually only be giving them half a tablet when they are smaller, and then the dose increases with their weight.

Some people recommend crushing the tablet and putting it in their food; while others prefer them to swallow the tablet whole. My only qualm with putting it in the food is that if the cat does not eat all of that meal, they will miss out on some of that dose of medication, so I prefer getting them to swallow the tablet. Also, many worm tablets are more effective when given on an empty stomach, so putting it in food is not ideal. Again, check the instructions on the packaging of your product.

Giving a cat a worm tablet is easier than you think, though I must admit that on my first try, I got my finger bitten. The important thing to remember is to be calm but firm. If you think you will get too nervous, get someone else to do it, or ask your vet to show you how to do it when you are there.

The simple procedure is: have the cat sitting on a raised, flat surface (table or coffee table) with their back against your tummy. Then with one hand, put your thumb and forefinger on either side of their mouth and gently prise their jaw open. With the other hand, drop the tablet onto the back of their tongue. Try to avoid putting your finger into their mouth to place the tablet because they will object and might try to bite your finger. Once the pill is in place on the back of the tongue, close their mouth and hold it closed for a few seconds while you gently rub their throat or blow on their nose to make them swallow. That's it, real simple!

Flea Treatment

Cats can pick up fleas, even if they live indoors full-time. The most straightforward form of flea treatment is a small tube of liquid that you squeeze on the back of their necks once a month. It is a very simple procedure,

The best way to administer flea treatment is to get someone to help you hold the cat secure. With one hand, spread the fur apart on the back of their head directly between their ears; then, with the other hand, hold the tube against their skin and squeeze it so that the liquid runs out onto their skin. A good tip: keep the tube squeezed as you pull it away from their skin, otherwise you might suck some of the liquid back up into the tube as you release your grip.

The cat might try and scratch at the liquid a bit while it dries, which is why you put it at the back of the head so that access to it is minimized. Also, you want to avoid touching the cat while the treatment is drying, and you don't want your kids to touch it. So it is advisable to do it at night, before bed, so that it is dry by the morning

Vaccinations

Your cat is also going to need be vaccinated to prevent getting a variety of common feline diseases, such as enteritis, parvovirus and cat flu. All cats need to be vaccinated regardless of whether they are an indoor or outdoor cat.

Your kitten will need to have three vaccination shots. The first one happens at about eight weeks old and will have already been given to them before you bought them. But for the next two shots, you will have to take them to the vet.

The second one is due at around twelve weeks, so it will probably need to happen soon after bringing them home. You may be able to get it done at the time of their first check-up visit, depending on their age when you acquire them. Then the third shot is then due at sixteen weeks.

Those first three shots will establish the immunity, and they will just need booster shots after that. The first booster is when they reach twelve months old, when they officially become an adult cat. Then, as an adult, they just require a booster shot every three years.

Vaccination Schedule:

1st shot at 6-8 weeks

2nd shot at 10-12 weeks

3rd shot at 14-16 weeks

Booster: 12 months

Booster: Every 36 months

De-sexing

De-sexing a pet cat is a must. The only reason for not de-sexing a cat would be if you were going to become a registered breeder.

There are some obvious advantages of de-sexing, such as the avoidance of unwanted pregnancies and the elimination of aggressive mating behavior. But there are also less understood health benefits such as the reduced likelihood of developing feline illnesses, such as uterus infections or breast cancer in females and prostate cancer in males.

What age?

The traditional age for getting a cat-desexed is around the five-and-half to six-month mark. But there are many pet care organizations now advocating early age de-sexing (EAD) at around eight to twelve weeks. The reason for this is that a cat reaches sexual maturity at around 4 months, and so your cat could start exhibiting behavioral problems from then.

Avoiding sex-drive related behavioral problems is one of the main reasons to get your cat de-sexed:

Female - A female cat on heat might start howling out loud, calling for a mate. You you might find male cats being attracted to your door or fighting near your home.

Male - A male cat might start spraying (urinating) around the home to mark their territory in rivalry with other male cats outside.

Either sex may try to escape the home to get out and find a mate. De-sexing a cat, therefore, makes them less like to roam and subsequently less likely to get run over by a car. So, whichever way you look at it, getting your cat de-sexed is a kind and helpful thing to do for them.

Surgery

De-sexing of a cat is done as a surgical procedure under general anesthetic at a veterinary clinic. It is a straightforward procedure, and your cat will fully recover after a few days. You should book your de-sexing appointment with your vet at one of your regular check-ups about a month prior.

Spaying - for a female cat, the de-sexing process is known as Spaying. It consists of removing the uterus and the ovaries through a small, half-inch incision on the belly. There will be some stitches, but often these will not be visible if the vet uses the "internal stitching" method.

Neutering – for a male cat, the de-sexing process is known as Neutering. It consists of removing the testes through a small incision in the scrotum. Stitches generally shouldn't be required.

What to expect

You will need to drop your cat off at the vet in the morning and pick them up later that afternoon. The vet will check your cat for general health, making sure they haven't got a cold or any other condition that could increase the risk of surgery. Then they will then administer the anesthetic and perform the de-sexing procedure. After that, they will monitor your cat as they recover and make sure that they are well enough to go home with you that evening.

Post-op Care

When you pick-up your cat from the vet after de-sexing, they might seem a little quiet and subdued if the anesthetic is still wearing off. Equally, though, you may also find them surprisingly happy and lively because they are on pain medication.

One thing that may come as a shock, if you are not expecting it, is that some of the hair on their belly will have been shaved. That beautiful thick coat they were growing now seems ruined! But don't worry, it's not. It will all grow back in a few weeks or so.

When you take them home, the vet will give you some pain killers to administer for the next few days. This may be in the form of pills, but it is more likely these days to be a small syringe of liquid which you can squirt into their food or directly into their mouth.

Don't fret. The fact the vet is giving you pain medication doesn't mean that your pet is feeling a lot of pain. It is just a preventative measure to stop them from feeling a little sore while the wound heals-over and is only to ensure their utmost comfort.

You will need to monitor them for about a week and check that the wound is healing nicely. As long as it is not weeping or turning red and getting hot, all is okay. If you do notice any redness or symptoms of infection, just call your vet, and they will advise you over the phone.

In any case, you will need to take them back to the vet for a ten-day check-up just to ensure that everything has gone well, and the wound has healed up nicely. That ten-day check-up should be a free appointment.

Chapter 10

Busting Common Cat Myths

"The problem with cats is that they get the same exact look whether they see a moth or an axe-murderer."

Paula Poundstone

OKAY, IT'S TIME FOR SOME FUN! You have no doubt heard many weird and wonderful so-called "facts" about cats. But are any of those things true? Or are they just old wives' tales? Let's have a look at some and find out...

Myth 1: Cats have nine lives

Do cats *really* have nine lives? It's a saying as old as the ages: "Cats have nine lives!" But is it true? Are cats like a video game character, able to spring back to life after being killed until all their lives are used up?

Of course not! Their reputation for having multiple lives is an exaggeration by us incredulous humans who marvel at seeing cats survive situations that would mean certain death for us.

Cats seem to be able to fall from anything, even great heights, and always land on their feet. They react and run so fast that they are able to get out of dangerous situations that would most likely cause us to meet our maker. This uncanny ability to get themselves out of trouble leaves us jealous that they are so agile and seem so "lucky," hence our judgment that they must have more than one life to use.

Myth busted? Yes! - Cats are just as mortal as humans, with only one life to live.

Myth 2: Cats can see in the dark

Can cats really see in the dark? At night, you can always spot a cat as their eyes glow like hot coals in the dark. But can they see you?

Well, actually, yes, they can! Cats are able to make out shapes very well in the dark. Here's the thing though, their eyesight is not better than ours; it is just different. Cats have about six times more optical rods in their retinas than humans do, making them much more sensitive to light, which enables them to clearly make out shapes in very low levels of light. Since they are so sensitive to light, they have vertically closing pupils that allow them to limit the amount of light entering their eyes in bright daylight.

Humans, on the other hand, have less retinal rods but many more cones in our retinas, which makes our color perception much better, but only in good daylight. We can also focus better at a distance than cats, with cats having to be five times closer to something to see it as clearly as we can.

But cats have the last laugh, though, because they are not going to stub their toe on the end of the bed in the dark!

Myth busted? No, it's true! - Cats CAN see much better in the dark than humans can!

Myth 3: Cats and Dogs hate each other

Do cats and dogs really dislike each other? We all watched cartoons when we were growing up, right? So we all know that cats and dogs are mortal enemies. Just about every cartoon ever created has expounded the theory that cats and dogs can't even be in the same room without needing to start a fight. But is that true? Is it really a thing?

No! The only real basis of this theory is that cats and dogs are both territorial animals and like to "own" their patch of ground. So seeing a dog or a cat chasing one another away is just the same as seeing one cat facing-off with another or one dog chasing away another dog.

When cats and dogs are first introduced to each other in the same household, they will initially be a little hostile to one another as they jostle for control of the domain. But once they have settled in and got used to each other being there, they get along really well. They get to accept each other as part of their family just like they accept you, and they become the best of friends. When cats and dogs live together, you will often see them playing together or cuddled-up together on the floor.

Myth busted? Yes! - There is no feline-vs-canine war; cats and dogs get on just fine!

Myth 4: Cats get high on Catnip

Do cats *really* love Catnip and get high on it? Another stereotype expressed by cartoons is that cats get high on Catnip and get addicted to it like some kind of narcotic drug. But is this true? What is Catnip anyway? And is it intoxicating? Well, kind of...

Catnip is a perennial herb that is part of the mint family. Cats generally dislike mint, which is a good thing, because many varieties contain salicylate, which is mildly poisonous to cats. But Catnip, on the other hand, although it is a type of mint, contains no salicylate at all. Instead, it contains an essential oil called Nepetalactone, and that is where the fun begins!

When a cat catches the fragrance of the Nepetalactone oil from a catnip plant, it is immediately attracted to the aroma. They love it. They will often start chewing it or rubbing themselves on it in an effort to release more of the oil. The Nepetalactone has an immediate intoxicating effect, which lasts about ten to fifteen minutes. During that time, your cat might behave one of two ways: either they become real mellow and blissed out, drooling and stretching and chilling out; or they became hyped-up and start jumping around in a frenzy of hyperactivity. Once the initial reaction has worn off, though, any further dose of catnip has no effect, and it takes a couple of hours or so before your cat becomes sensitive to it again.

Another thing to keep in mind is that *not all* cats are affected by the lure of catnip. Kittens are generally not affected by it, as they have not yet developed the sensitivity to it. And even when they are older, only about two-thirds of adult cats react to it. So don't be dismayed if your cat doesn't go crazy over it.

Myth busted? No! - Many cats DO love catnip and get intoxicated by it.

Myth 5: Cats are scared of cucumbers

Cats scared of *cucumbers*? What am I talking about?

Well, if you haven't been on YouTube for a while, just type in the word cat and the word cucumber, and you will see what I mean. A quick search will bring up hundreds of videos of people placing cucumbers on the ground behind their cat while it is eating, then laughing at the cat's behavior when it turns around and sees it. The

SMITTEN BY KITTEN

most common reaction is that the cat totally freaks out, jumps high into the air in fright, and runs away as fast as possible.

So what is it that the cat is scared of? Are they actually afraid of the cucumber itself, or is it something else? Well, the answer is that no one really knows! The cat experts are still yet to agree on a definitive answer.

Some believe that since the cucumber is a long thin shape, the cat thinks it is a snake. In the wild, a snake presents a significant life-or-death danger for a cat. So just turning around to see a snake-like shape right next to them is enough to trigger an instinctive reaction, causing the cat to leap clear of any possible venom strike.

This explanation makes sense to me, as I know that cats react instinctively to a lot of things, just based on shape. They grab at anything that dangles; they chase torchlight on the floor or walls; they spin in circles chasing their tails – all without thinking, just automatically reacting to the visual shapes they see. So reacting to a snake-like shape seems reasonable.

Others believe that it is just the element of surprise that causes the reaction. All these videos show people sneaking up on their cats whilst they are preoccupied, eating. When a cat is eating, it is at its most vulnerable to being attacked. Its head is down in the bowl, and it is unable to monitor the space around it for predators. So it is thought that when a cat looks up and finds something right behind it that was not there a few minutes ago, it gets a genuine surprise and feels that vulnerability, and reacts accordingly. This could also be true; we just don't know for sure.

So should you try this out for yourself at home? Well, you can, but I wouldn't recommend it. While it sounds like fun, it is a pretty mean trick to play on your poor, unsuspecting, beloved little friend. Sure your big brother may have played tricks on you when you were growing up - but did *you* actually *enjoy* that? And there could be consequences too. As well as the shock, the immediate adrenaline surge, and the high heart rate due to the fight-or-flight reaction, you also risk causing them long-term anxiety and stress. If you do it too often, they might become anxious about eating or become too scared to be in the room where you played the prank. And that, in turn, could lead to problems with not using the litter tray, etc. Hmm, maybe it's better just to be kind to them.

Myth busted? Maybe! – The jury is still out on this one.

Myth 6: Cats love to drink Milk

Pretty much every children's TV show I watched growing-up, suggested that if a stray cat comes to your door, you should give it a saucer of milk. Is that correct? Do cats like to drink milk?

Well, they do, but they shouldn't! They *will* drink it if you put it in front of them because it is high in fat and will taste rich and creamy, but they are not able to digest it properly. Giving them cow's milk will most likely give them an upset stomach and cause mild diarrhea.

They can tolerate and digest their mother's milk when they are young, but once they have been weaned, they stop producing the enzymes necessary to break down lactose and hence are essentially lactose intolerant. So, the best thing for cats to drink, at any age, is water.

Myth busted? Yes! - You should not give milk to cats.

SO, THERE ARE MANY MYTHS about cats and their behavior, but few of them are true. The existence of these myths is most likely because humans find cats so mysterious. We see their behavior as so different from ours that we try and find a way to explain it without really understanding them. After all, we are not cats! I am sure that cats look at us, humans, and find us just as mysterious and bewildering.

Afterword

In Summary

Well, surely, after all that you have read, you should be of the same opinion as me by now: that cats are beautiful creatures and make ideal pets!

Anyone of any age can benefit from having a cat as a companion. Their graceful nature can influence our mood to calm us down and make us feel loved, and give us an object to focus our love on. From the youngest to the oldest, we can all appreciate the benefits of owning a cat, and anyone can fall in love with a feline friend.

When you decide to buy a cat, it is best to plan the purchase carefully: choose a breed, talk to breeders or pet shops in your local area, and ideally, wait for a new litter to be born and weaned. When you choose a kitten, make personality the deciding factor rather than looks, and try to pick a kitten that you feel drawn to and connect with. Before you bring them home, prepare your home just as carefully as if you were bringing home a newborn human baby: remove all dangers and work out the best place for food bowls, bed, litter box, etc.

Health-wise, always have your new pet checked by your local vet within the first few days and then visit the vet regularly for vaccinations and check-ups. Make sure you get your cat de-sexed in the first 4 to 6 months and make sure you administer flea treatments and worm tablets at the required intervals. Looking after your cat like this will ensure they are always in the best of health and live a long and happy life with you and your family.

Apart from those obvious healthcare costs, a cat is a relatively low-maintenance animal to own as a pet. There is generally no bathing required, as they clean themselves. There is no daily walking needed, as they exercise themselves. There is minimal cleaning-up after them, as they use a litter tray. There is no forgetting to feed them, as they will always come and remind you that it is meal time. For such a low investment in time and energy output required, you get a great return in the high level of attention and affection they give you.

For the environmentally conscious, I have also read that cats are far more environmentally-friendly than dogs to own and maintain. As far as greenhouse gas emissions go, keeping a dog has been compared to owning a large 4-weel drive vehicle, whereas keeping a cat can be compared to owning a small hatchback.

Whichever way you look at it, owning a cat is a delightful and rewarding experience. You are never alone when you own a cat. There is a kitten out there for everyone. And somewhere, there is a kitten waiting to be loved by you!

So what are you waiting for? Get out there and GET SMITTEN!

Leave a Review

Customer Reviews

★★★★★ 2
5.0 out of 5 stars ▾

5 star		100%
4 star		0%
3 star		0%
2 star		0%
1 star		0%

See all verified purchase reviews ›

Share your thoughts with other customers

Write a customer review

I would be incredibly grateful if you could take 60 seconds to leave a quick review on Amazon, even if it's just a line or two!

Thank you!

References

Ref [1] Page 10

Cheryl M. Straede & Richard G. Gates M.D. (1993) Psychological Health in a Population of Australian Cat Owners, Anthrozoös, 6:1, 30-42, DOI: 10.2752/089279393787002385

Ref [2] Page 11

International Stroke Conference 2008, New Orleans, Feb. 20-22, 2008. Farhan Siddiq, MD, University of Minnesota, Minneapolis. Daniel Lackland, MD, spokesman, American Stroke Association; professor of epidemiology, Medical University of South Carolina, Charleston.

Ref [3] Page 11

DR Ownby et al. Exposure to dogs and cats in the first year of life and risk of allergic sensitization at 6 to 7 years of age. Journal of the American Medical Association 288(8): 963-72 (2002).

Ref [4] Page 12 & Ref [5] Page 88

The Journal of the Acoustical Society of America 110, 2666 (2001); https://doi.org/10.1121/1.4777098

Jenssen Books

Printed in Great Britain
by Amazon

75174996R00092